KNOW how to show support
When you feel <u>NO</u> Support.

"You have to be willing to let other people help you. Ask for support and allow yourself to be supported".

-Iyanla Vanzant

Copyright 2020 Brodie Proctor
ALL RIGHT RESERVED
ISBN: 78-0-578-71207-9

In Loving Memory

Lewis G Taylor III (FATHER)
Carol Y Proctor (GRANDMOTHER)
Elizabeth Taylor (SISTER)
Allison Proctor (AUNT)
Alexis Demby (BEST FRIEND)

"This book has definitely made me have self-reflection. I loved the emotion of pictures being painted in my mind, as I continuously read through. The analogies in this book will definitely be a wakeup call for those lost in the world of social media awareness while losing sight of those around us literally versus virtually, and challenge everyone to be the friend they want to have."
#RodMingerSaidIt

-Rod Minger, Actor/Comedian

"This was a beautiful Saturday afternoon SELF CHECK moment. This reiterated that this LIFE is NOT ALL ABOUT ME! The days I'm strong I can use that to help others and the days I'm weak I can reach out and simply ask for help! Brodie this is thought provoking and an easy read! Congratulations Friend!"

-Brely Evans, Actor/Producer

"Support from others are like building blocks to your journey. In whatever stage in life you're in, your Support System is essential. As per me, I look to my village for advice, encouragement, an ear, a shoulder to cry on, and Quality time -My Love Language! When I need my Wooosah moments I look to my Support system to help me breathe!!! Being supported and of Support to someone can make a major difference in someone's life. God created us all to be a helping hand and a help meet to one another! Love Thy Neighbor as you love yourself! That's Bible so we should all try our best to stand on it!"

-Y'Anna Crawley, Singer/Songwriter & Author

"This book is good!!
Don't expect you from other people. To have a successful relationship with anyone require communication and reciprocation."

-Jocelyn McCoy-Brown, Life Coach

TABLE OF CONTENTS

FOREWORD

1. WHAT IS SUPPORT?
2. CHILD SUPPORT
3. TOXIC SUPPORT
4. LOVING SUPPORT
5. UNDERSTANDING SUPPORT
6. GODLY SUPPORT
7. YOU SUPPORT

FOREWORD:

From escorting me to my sweet sixteen and attending my dance shows as teenagers, to deep conversations about the struggles of life over a glass of wine in our adulthood, Brodie has always been an extremely supportive friend. I have known Brodie for more than half of my life, he is truly my most trusted confidant. I know that if I call him, whether it's to chat and catch up or to vent about a troubling situation, he would be there for me to give me the support and advice that I need, even if it is something that I don't want to hear, I know that it is coming from a place of love. But what happens when the person you care for needs you in a way that you aren't sure you can deliver?

Under uncertain circumstances, in your darkest moments, and during your most difficult times, support is paramount and crucial. In his debut self-help book, Brodie took a brave step to share how he has come to *Know Support* to make it through his most challenging experiences. Brodie has always been a person who will put himself last for the sake of caring for and supporting others. But at some point, this type of helpfulness took a toll on him, as his own challenging situations started to stack up and impact him in such a profound way. During this turning point in his life, he had to figure out how to work through those challenges and seek out the proper support for himself in order to make it out of this seemingly unending downward spiral. Know Support is a great self-help book that offers some valuable gems about how to give and receive support. It opens the door to a sometimes uncomfortable conversation that should have been had, but maybe we're too scared to start. More importantly, it gives an honest look into the different types of support that everyone needs.

Adalena Baxter, M.S., LBS

Chapter 1: What is Support?

Sup-port

Verb

1. Bear all or part of the weight of; hold up.

2. Provide assistance to, especially financially; enable to function or act.

Noun

1. A thing that bears the weight of something or keeps it upright.

2. Material assistance.

Support is something you always need but don't always know how to provide or even know how to receive it.

We are in dire need whether you realize or not. It is a desire deep down that not all can fulfill. Support is something we need to survive even if we do not want to be honest with our self. We often live in a place of denial on how much we need people around us to support us in many ways.

Here are some examples and break down of types and ways to offer support.

Physical support

Have you experienced a time where you were in an accident and broke a leg? Or, in my case jumped down the stairs running a beating from my dear loving mother and fractured my leg. (Now, it is funny to recall that moment, but it was not so funny on that instance).

So, from that event, I realized how I needed physical support. I needed help getting around or up and down from the couch. As much as we find it uncomfortable to ask, we have to be honest with ourselves and KNOW we NEED help.

Most of us at some point in time had to be taken care of physically in some type of way.

From birth, we are unable to tend to ourselves and we have no choice but to rely on someone, often our parents to help us grow and flourish as they provide us with the necessary support to thrive in this world.

Our first experiences with support are reflected through the support of our caretakers with food. By supporting us with a roof over our head, they supported us at least with the basic necessities. This type of support provides us with the things we need to survive. The lack of basic support in our early years of life can sometimes impact us more than we realize later in life.

As we continue to grow from toddler into our teenage years, we begin seeking support in other ways. Either through our actions of joining some sort of group, be it a sports team, band, or even a dance group. In our experiences in these groups, we look forward to rallying with other people that are coming to cheer us on. Whether it is backstage at the recital or game day, we look out for our friends or parents to make sure they are present. Feeling and seeing that support is much needed and impactful.

Unfortunately, when we do not feel as though we are not receiving that support, this feeling in our gut of disappointment sticks with us. Many start building up a tolerance as if we then don't need them to be there to avoid being disappointed. I am very guilty of this myself as I stopped looking for people who would show up. I stopped having expectations of people showing up for me because I did not want them to let me down. As the saying goes: "Don't get your hopes too high."

However, something I have learned to live by is ...

No Expectations = No Disappointments

Allow me to ask a few questions and have you ponder a moment.

When do you think support is needed? Do you ever feel like there is a wrong time to provide or show support?

Support, supporting or being supported is not always easy! - Sometimes taking a step back and letting those around us learn on their own is the most difficult best thing to ever do at times.

Not being a crutch might be the best thing someone needs at times. However, I do believe we should voice how or what we feel and let them know what our position is so when they do learn what they need to learn during that time, they can stand tall and come and say thank you and appreciate you and not hold resentment forever.

Emotional Support

This is something that is not easy for many! I have a cousin that is so detached from his feelings that being there for you emotional is not his strong suit. You being overly emotional tends to leave him confused on what to do or say in that time. So, let me try and help others who may also find themselves in that situation.

A simple, "Are you ok?" can really go a long way! Trust me!

A person may not need you to sit and cry with them or be irate as alongside them. Simply hearing a person vent or talk through their emotions might be all they need.

So let's think for a moment, when was the last time you called to simply say "Hello, how are you feeling? Truly?

When was the last time you called to only hear how they are doing and not unload your problems?

Now that you thought about it and perhaps are unable to remember the last time, try it from time to time.

Let's also flip this and take a moment to think about when was the last time someone did call to ask how you were. How did you answer? Did you let them know you may have not been okay? That you have been dealing with a lot and not knowing how to handle it all? Many of us feel we cannot share our problems because we will come with many. So we tend to just think it is pointless to even share our headache or heartache. That isn't fair to yourself or is fair to that person that really may genuinely be wanting or trying to be there for you. Give them a chance.

In 2019, for example, I went through a very traumatic emotional event and it left me in a space where I felt I was all alone and had no one to confide in or to share my daily struggles. I was fighting to hold on to life. I was fighting to hold my head up. I laid in bed many days and did not want to move. To be honest, at times, I didn't know if I even wanted to wake. I went through so much at one time and I would prayed that God could just take me away from this pain, take me from the place I felt was like hell.

I had one client I was doing some work for and the only days I would leave my house was to attend an event with her. It used to take me all day sometimes to pull myself together to put on a smile to face the world and pretend I was okay. I don't even know If she realized how down and out I was because I mastered my poker face.

I mastered my poker face and would pretend I was okay because deep down in my heart I felt as if no one even cared.

I felt this way mainly because they didn't call to check on me, so I was sure there was no way they could care. I soon learned that was a lie. A lie I was so desperately trying to hold on to because I started to become comfortable in this place of depression. I became okay with not being okay. In my mind, I felt it was okay to keep not wanting to be okay.

One thing I learned was ...

I couldn't

heal because I kept pretending

I wasn't hurt.

Many people always thought of me as the strong friend and I was the one always okay.

NEWS FLASH!!!
Your strong friends have weak moments as well!

They are not always okay! They may need a check in call sometimes.

If they happen to share with you they are not okay, don't go deep diving in your problems. Allow them ease into and open up. Just be sure to be a listening ear when they need you.

Show interest in their life outside of whatever they might be struggling with. Show that you care, and they might trust you more to open up later.

Stop by with their favorite treat or wine. Share some encouraging words. Little sweet gestures will go far and they will remember during the thoughts that will race through their head when alone.

So regardless how detached you may be from emotions or how much that is not something you are accustomed to, join me in trying to reach those we have not heard from. Reach out to those that maybe gave a short and quick answer the last time you called to check on them.

Try to do something that is out of your comfort zone.

Stop worrying about whether it will be uncomfortable for you and reach out to do something that you might not normally do.

Take a moment and ask yourself, do you have people around you who can vent and get a good cry out? And if you don't, this can easily lead to why we need the following support.

Mental support

Mental health issues are often ignored or overlooked to the outsider, so it is difficult for those of us that "suffer" to talk about them. The outsider often may think we simply need to pull up our bootstraps and cope, while we feel like it is entirely out of our control.

It's not as if I want to feel like this. Not as if I want to feel like life is not worth living. So, just saying "Man up" isn't always that easy! It is not so easy to just "get over it".

And to you whom has dealt with mental struggles...Do you know when or if you need mental support? Are you aware of your full mental state?

And, do you know your own triggers? Honestly aware? If not, have you ever sought out help or someone to discuss this with? If not, first forget about the shame that society tries to place on seeking mental health assistance such as a psychiatrist, therapist or even a life coach. People need to grow up and let people do what is best for them and let them heal properly without any added judgement.

What does that look like for you supporting someone dealing with mental illness in any capacity?

Remember to never deal with a person as if the illness does not exist as I had a close family member that dealt with mental illness.

Indeed, that was the hardest thing for me to try and understand. Understand that I can't simply talk to them like the person that they once were.

And being fully transparent, I never fully got that! So no where am I saying it is easy but it's something we should work on daily and strive for, especially for the one that needs us. They are dealing with many issues and warring with themselves. Get to a point in which you can express what support you need.

When I was in the midst of everything I was dealing with, I had to be sure to seek out a therapist and see her more than regular. I was going about twice a week to help pull me out of the sunken place I was in. I was sharing this and stopped feeling ashamed of needed to talk through this. However, I didn't let society stop me from receiving the proper mental support that I knew I needed!

Chapter 2: Child Support

Earlier in the book I spoke about a child needing physical support. Let's touch on how else a child may need your support. And in this chapter of life, it's not about financial related matters.

Growing up, did you ever feel that you could truly be who or whatever you wanted to be? Did the person raising you invested in your dreams and passions and try to help manifest them?

Message for parents, your children needs to hear "well done" "I am proud of you" sometimes! Words of affirmation may not be your strong love language, but it certainly needs to be every now and again.

When I was younger, I was blessed to have a mother that would support my dreams! Whatever I wanted to do, she was right there trying to make it happen. Even when and after I said I wanted to learn the piano and quit shortly after her buying me the complete piano set, she still pushed me to find my passion.

Did you feel your parents supported your dreams and aspirations? Did they come to your recitals, sports games, concerts, talent shows, Parent Teacher Conferences?

Did you look for them to be there ? Or, were you okay because they worked so much? And if they did make it to all your events... How do you feel that helped you in life?

I had to be honest with myself as much as I loved how much support my mother showed me, it set me up for false expectations of the world. I grew up thinking everyone would support me like that. I felt everyone was just as passionate as I was about my visions and dreams. I learned very quickly that was not the case.

So parents, single or married, many had to work... Did you do your part on explaining why you missed things because of work?

Did you fully explain how the household worked and the work schedule that was in place?

Did you explain why you were or not able to be there to pick them up or drop them off to or from school?

We have to give our children more credit and help them understand the ins and outs of how their life is affected by every decision you make for them. I feel at times we assume a child will just understand. They will be okay with whatever you decide as a parent because we know best!

So, when I was younger my older brother asked me to be his second child's godfather so I accepted the role, knowing how serious it is to be a godparent. I have certain standards because I always knew what I wanted and what I expected from my godparents so I wanted to exude that same energy. I wanted to show that same compassion, love, and support that I wanted from my godparents which sadly I did not always receive. I had to work through that in my life's journey, but I never wanted a child that called me godfather to experience those same feelings. So, I always wanted to make sure I was doing my part. Yes, it was difficult! While he was younger in school, I made sure he had his favorite things at the same time making sure he obtained good grades. I made it very clear if he was unable to do his job at school, I could not reward him for that. No one gets a bonus at work if their performance is poor.

I do not understand why any child thinks I should buy anything special or do for them anything extra or go out of my way to make you are more comfortable in life if you can't simply do well in school. I did my part and fully explained that and received many report cards full of A's!

I strongly feel if you bring me home basic grades you will have your basic needs. And, I you don't want to do any extra in school, you are not putting in any extra time or energy in it, neither am I on things that you want. No sir!

I come from a family of 13 siblings, and my godson happens to also be my nephew. I always did for him as my godson though! So on one occasion, one of my lovely siblings heard that I was buying my godson a pair of sneakers for school and they reached out and said well your other nephew needs some pair of shoes and it took me by surprise because I was never buying for my nephew, I was buying it for my godchild. I thought that was clear. Needless to mention, I have many nieces and nephews. I think I'm up to 19 or 20, so many I have truly lost count! I knew early on I could support their children in that way so I never wanted to set that tone. So, I stayed fair and neutral with them all. I will as an uncle participate in group activities, but if I cannot buy 20 pairs of sneakers, I wasn't buying any!

To this date, I have no children and I didn't agree to have 20 kids to support. I will give my love and energy when I am there or in town as much as I can, but material things I made clear I can only do for my godchild to just be fair across-the-board. I never wanted to come across as the unfair uncle because I have experienced that firsthand and it's not a good feeling. There are so many birthday's or something coming up I would be living a ramen noodle life if I was trying to do all of them.

I chose not to have kids so I could enjoy my life a little more. I know how selfish I am, so from that I had to explain to her why I could not do that. In the capacity she was asking, I could not be of assistance.

I had to break things down to her and explain why my "nephew" was getting this or the other not because he was my nephew, but because he was my godchild. Now, she was able to understand or perhaps not, but one thing I always made clear was that if her household needed help I would help her out. I am not going to allow my siblings or nieces or nephews to be in the dark if I am able to help.

I will not allow my family not to have food if I can help. I will not allow my family to be on the street if I can help. So, if you ask me at a time that I'm able to help, I will do just that. I will support and encourage you as much as I can.

I will help as my family, but I cannot just buy something extra or materialistic items because you feel I should and especially not on your time. I will support you as my family in a time of need. I will support you if I can. I always try to make that clear to my family. Yes, I may live hundreds of miles away, I may be busy for the majority of my life, but I will never see my family go without if there's something I can do to help my family. We all need help at some point.

Chapter 3: Toxic Support

There were many times I would sit up and just wonder, am I really someone that has friends? Am I really someone that has a family or am I someone that is part of a community because at those moments by myself I felt so alone?

I felt like I had no one. I felt as if no one had my back. I felt I had no one to call and to lean on. It was difficult when times came that I felt as though I had no shoulder to cry on. Even during those times, I didn't have a hand to help me move or hang a picture or rearrange my living room or any of those simple acts of service.

Was it me pushing them away? Was it me putting up a brick wall? Was it me not allowing them in or showing them that I needed help? Honestly, I thought I was showing I needed help but maybe I wasn't. I just always went back-and-forth in my mind saying, am I doing enough to show I need help or am I not receiving the support that I needed?

I had to wonder if it was okay to visit my friends that were MIA and making sure they are okay. Sometimes you have to check yourself, look in the mirror and self-evaluate.

Support is not always something that you think you need or desire, but it's like air; we have to have it. You have to have the support to get through the tough times, the rough times, the sad times, the moments when you do feel alone and in need of that support from whomever you call friend or family. You deserve that support.

Never allow people to think that asking for support makes you lower than them or that it is inadequate to ask for it or that you need help and support. You will know when you need help as it is awareness of yourself to say I need you to survive like the song says.

I won't harm you with words from my mouth, you know people have been harmed because they needed support and we didn't give our friend the right support or the right answer or the hug at the time they needed it. We turned our back on them, we rushed off the phone to something that probably was not important. We were too busy scrolling down Instagram and not listening to our friends in despair. How many times can we say we have been guilty of that? This generation has been so busy and wrapped up into people's lives on social media and ignoring the importance of the lives that are in our faces, our homes, our churches, our jobs, our social settings and we say those are the people that matter and love. We often say those are the people we care about, but we spend the majority of our day checking on people in this virtual world that can care less about what we are doing. We care so much about people that we have not reached to or are not in touch if they have a death in the family.

Rather, we are sending them well wishes and DM's and try to make sure they know we are showing their love and support to them but are we doing that for the people that are in our space that are in arm's reach that actually need our compassion and sympathy and empathy during that half grieving moment? Are we showing up?

Are we showing we care? Let's take a moment and ponder that and ask ourselves we can say we care all day long, we can say we are there for you, but do our actions convey that? Do our actions speak louder than our words? That's what we look for from other people so are we holding ourselves to the same standards? Are we holding ourselves accountable? Are we holding a mirror and saying am I being that friend that I want in return? Am I being a support system that I always desire and need it in my life? Who am I in a time that my friend needs me? Who am I at a time when my friend lost their job? Who am I with my friend who just had a miscarriage?

Who am I when my child just got dumped for the first time and thought that was the love of your life? Who am I at times like that?

Are you like many people who don't want people simply call them when they need them? We want people to just call us to talk or hear us, but are we always calling to check on them before we need something? Are we calling that random person to make sure they are okay before or are we quick to check the other person to put a pause in the conversation to let them know that's not the way. Have you ever stop to think has something been going on that caused us not to talk?

Has something going on that may prevent them to be able to reach out as something big going on that they were not ready to share. Was something going on that had them in a bad headspace and they did not feel like I may have the time or patience to sit and listen and help them through it? Do we ever stop and think of it from that angle instead of jumping to the illusion that they are only calling when they need something? They might be calling because they are at the end of their rope and needed their lifeline and that lifeline was you. They felt you were the person that could help them through. They thought you were the person that would hold or help lift them up or help them pick themselves up by their bootstraps.

They thought you were going to be there back bone at that time and not judge them for maybe being MIA without knowing what caused them to be missing.

What do you do after you tell someone how do you expect to be supportive and ask them for help along the way? And they say oh yeah I'm here for you whenever you need and then when you need them and feel like they are nowhere to be found. What do you do when you thought someone you can always count on moves on and has new friends and a new relationship, has kids, a new family a new home a new job? And do you feel lost under all their sauce, what do you do? Do you remove yourself? Do you fight for that place in their life?

Do you bring it up to them? Now, say you bring it up and they brush it off, how are you supposed to react? Do you argue them down? Do you tell them that their new relationship or new promotion that they always wanted is getting in the way of your friendship? Do you tell them that their kids are taking up all the time and you feel slighted is that selfish to say. So, we have to realize when it's being selfish or is it being realistic and then ask ourselves is it wrong to be selfish when one name a place in our friends heart is a selfish to want your mother to be your mother even when she's moved on and may have remarried? How do you tell her, mom I still need you, we have to ask ourselves these questions to reevaluate our feelings towards the people we love.

The people we call friends, the people that are our significant others, even to our kids. Are you making sure your relationship is priority and that you are conveying it? So, it's clear where you all stand it's not fair to either party to let someone live in a great area or for you to be left in a great area you either love me and you support me or we need to work through this and figure out some type of middle ground. However, we should never feel bad or feeling like we need to address the situation at hand. We have to make sure we are not living behind a wall and not expressing ourselves for me we have to make sure that our heart is not being shipped or where our heart comes first. We have to make sure we are being treated like we wish.

We have to make sure we are treating others the same way we always see the golden rule; treat others the way we want to be treated. Do we really wholeheartedly honestly live by that do we uphold that statement on a day-to-day basis? Do we treat our children like we want to be treated? Do we treat our bosses like we want to be treated? Do we treat the person that we are lying in bed next to you every night like we want to be treated every day? I would have to admit I'm guilty of not treating people in my life the way I really wanted to be treated, but I expected them to treat me right.

Some of us haven't cried for ourselves because too many people are crying out to us every day.

You haven't been able to shoulder your own problems because you have been too busy being a shoulder for others . Sometimes you have to use what you have to lift yourself up. Let me drop this here for you to put some things into perspective, I saw someone post during the pandemic that people that didn't call and check up on them WERE TAKING NOTICE!

I sat and stared there a bit and was so perplexed that nowhere in there did they wonder what has made them not able to reach out to us or check on us or maybe they were handling this pandemic differently. Perhaps they had situations of loss and we are not even able to have the option of going to an actual funeral.

I lost a really dear friend of mine in the beginning of the pandemic. It really hit hard when finding out that the only option was cremation which left us no option to view or see the body one last time, knowing that I was unable to see him because of what's been going on and not doing so even one last time.

I dealt with that with no one around because we were QUARANTINING! So, when you don't hear from someone that is your friend, stop and think why were they maybe not able to reach out to you or tell you what was going on. They can't always be the one checking on you.

I may have been handling things one way, but you're over there fine and everything is going just peachy and cream and upset that I didn't give out of my grief, but you are not wondering what might going on with me. We have to stop allowing ourselves in our minds to play that trick on us and form walls of hostility and walls of hatred and walls of separation to get between people that we know deep in our hearts love us and understand that everyone has a life.

Everyone handles their day-to-day life differently. There are many things that we go through on a daily basis that we deal with internally.

We have to work on understanding that your good friend has an entire husband and that is not what you signed up for, but sometimes you have to know that it is hard to sit and chit chat and talk and whine down on the phone with a friend like you used to for hours at a time.

As per me, I know that I do love you and support you through it all, whatever is going on whatever will arise I'm there for you. I got you like ISSA in Insecure "We Got Y'all".

Don't allow that toxic energy to be in your life.

Chapter 4: Loving Support

Do you understand if they can't make it? Do you share how you do expect them to honestly attempt to be there? And on you, do you make it clear you want them to be there and that it matters?

I have made that mistake many times of not making it plain how much it meant to see their face in the building and then missed the opportunity.

SUPPORTING COST?

What happens when you can't afford it? Or, feel like you cannot afford it? What does this conversation look like to you? Are you good with admitting when it is not in your current budget?

Time after time I did not have it to spend so I would not say anything nor purchase the item or patronize the service. So, it made me look unsupportive. All the while, I could have simply said "Hey Friend, I ain't got."

Let me try and work in budget next month or so and I will gladly support. How about its something you'd ever pay for or something you do not personally like for yourself. What to do next?

SHARE! SHARE! SHARE!

Share via Social media. Repost the marketing flyer that friend worked hard on putting together or spent money to have it made. We are so quick to repost something our "Friend in our HEAD" Celeb's product and rant and rave about it when we clearly know we cannot afford it!

And now not being able to purchase their item. We make video after video of us wearing or using the product. We post it time and time again with clever captions and all the hashtags in the world to boost this thing.

Have you ever put in this same energy for your dear friend sitting on the couch right now? Have you helped boost their company or product like you do for people you don't know and may NEVER know. I always try to support people around me as if it were my own company, my own product. Repost and share without them asking. Let's stop saying we can't afford to support and let's figure out how to support within our means.

Transparency about your need or desire to support.

Share via your coworkers or family.

When you are at work and you hear your coworker hired a cleaning service online, do you tell them that your friend has their own cleaning company? Do you tell them that they are the best in town?

Now, listen here- For those of you have a friend who are a business owner! Treat those who are referring your business right. TREAT them so well so they go back to work and be so thankful you told them about their cleaning service.

Chapter 5: Understanding Support

Should you have to ask for support? Do you feel it should just be known to your friends when and what to support? Even if we don't fully communicate the support that is needed or desired.

So, if someone in your life purchases your new sock line or new lip glass, but they don't go on IG to brag about it like they do all the celebrities, do you care? If it bothered you, would you feel comfortable saying something?

And now let's flip it, What if they post your product and always ask about it? They like all the posts you post, but never purchase it themselves? Then you see that they just bought some new lip gloss from MAC? What do you do or say? Do you address it? WITHOUT a "LOL" at the end?

We have to learn to be open and be transparent with our feelings. Transparent on how we truly feel!.

SUPPORT YOUR FRIENDS LIKE YOU DO WITH THESE CELEBRITIES YOU DON'T KNOW

You are having a major event that you have been planning out for months. You have posted the flyer on all your social media platforms and sent individual texts. You have noticed that your response rate is very low. As if people that normally see every text message for whatever reason are not seeing your message now. As this happens, it definitely starts to make you scratch your head and ponder what is really going on?

Your singing lead on Sunday at church...

You mention it to your friends and for whatever reason they cannot make it. Now, you are the friend that always goes out of their way to make it every event and always so face it when they mention it.

Chapter 6: Godly Support

"What I've discovered is that intimate connection and communication with my creator will always get me through because I know my support, my help, is just a prayer away. Release and detach from every person, every circumstance, every condition, and every situation that no longer serves a divine purpose in your life."
- Iyanla Canzant

Sometimes you just lay across your bed in the middle of the day and realize you have not been invited over and nowhere you haven't been invited to someplace that you usually go and wonder what have you done. What did they do? Did you offend them or was it just a mishap and communication, but sometimes during those idle time is when you need to just self-evaluate what is important and learn how to put the time with yourself as a priority. Value the time. Earlier this year, we went through quarantine dealing with the viral outbreak of COVID-19 and we thought at first, oh this is so horrible. What am I going to do?

How do I just stay in the house? How has God allowed this?

All of that, but I think during that time God was working on us. God was trying to talk to us. God was trying to build and strengthen the relationship that many of us have a lead slip to the side. We were keeping up with appearances as we trusted and believed, but we were figuring things out on our own because we were hustling and trying to figure out everything for ourselves, but God said I'm going to put you in a place that you can only depend on me. I think we learned that during the quarantine, time to wholeheartedly completely trust and believe that God is God and God is our provider and he is the one that truly supports us supporters each and every day.

In every situation, yeah we expect the support that we should be expecting from God from so many other people. We expect that love and support to come from everybody else when God is saying, I'm OK by myself I am the Lord of lords. And we say, oh yeah I know that I am not taking away from God, am I taking away from his power. I'm not taken with miss train, but yet when we get into a tough situation financially or anything else, we usually cold out who can help who. Can I borrow from? Who can loan me this? How can I fix it? How can I figure this out? Why are you trying to figure it out God already worked it out why are you trying to find out where the money comes from when God has more power and strength in his hands.

He's blessed you with every job, every company, every position that he's placed you in. No matter if jobs are closed and what situation, he still made a way out of no way in still supplied all of our needs and made sure we were eligible for forbearance on different bills and collectors and companies. He worked with us unusually and we probably should not even been worthy of it. He allowed rent companies to waive all fees and say just pay when you have it when that's never an option. He allowed us to always have food during that time. He allowed us to have peace of mind if we just stopped and said God I trust you, God I thank you.

We got to start walking towards our destiny with our head up high and knowing that what God has promised is coming whether people believe it or not. Whether people have your back, stand with you, help you write the plan if they don't. It's OK, God told Noah to build the arc and everyone laughed at him, but look how that turned out so whatever God puts in your heart for you to do whatever moves you whatever wakes you up. Whatever motivates you, keep going after it day in and day out. Don't stop reaching towards that mark.

Chapter 7: You Support

Sometimes you have to support yourself! Believe in yourself!

I recently heard a conversation which made me think hard. Issa Rae, who we know to be one of the top producers, writers, and actresses in the game right now and is crushing it on many different platforms such as movies on HBO, started off doing a YouTube series for four years and barely anybody knew who she was. It was not top-quality, but she was KEYWORD consistent. She went after it every week and did not give up and she came out of it with an HBO contract not some mediocre network. Not a place on TV that no one watches. No, she got a contract with a premium network channel that you have to pay extra to access because top notch shows and top-notch actors and actresses are on these platforms. Some awkward black girl from YouTube. If you don't believe consistency is key, then I don't know what it is. I don't know what to tell you if staying at something until a manifest that's all we need to look and model after.

Stick to it, stay the course and it's only a matter of time that the right person, at the right time will see what you are doing and now we can make something out of this. We can take these ideas and make something so much bigger. We can then grow and get approved for five seasons.

We often think, oh I'm working as a caregiver or even an Assistant to someone. There are people that will make you feel like you are supporting the person above you.

Supporting who's on top of you. Supporting who is managing you. Supporting who is cutting your paychecks. Supporting who you are bathing or changing or washing their hair or taking care of them

To be honest...

Sometimes that's the support we need, sometimes it's not about what we are doing for them, but sometimes it's what it's doing for us! How it is causing us to grow! How it's grooming us! How it's making us a better person! How it's making us stronger. How it's making us flatter footed! How it's helping us make a better decision! How it makes us stay focused and in that humble place so when our dreams and goals and visions start manifesting, we know how to handle it, we will know how to carry it. You will you know how to stick to it. We will know how to stay determined because we've done the grunt work we've done it for other people and now we get to turnaround and do it for ourselves.

In life we are exposed to things to get us prepared for what's in store for us. People work in different fields and learn different things not knowing that one day that's going to be something we need to incorporate in our life. You can be living in a low cost area and push yourself to become a realtor and find clients that are in the place to buy a million dollar home and want you to broker the deal for them and now you are exposed to all these different homes and different areas. Now, you are privileged to know all the ins and outs of these homes and what makes you think or believe that it is something that maybe is for you. Now, you are exposed to and learn what you may really want in a home, what you don't like what you may want to build or what you may want to add to a home and you now have inside information on when the market is right. You now know when is a good time to buy a house. You now are the right person to talk to and you now have the room to broker your own house so that's just an example of what may come if you work in a certain field but may not be there at this current time. Don't look at it saying oh this is a torture. Don't look at this, is it not fair or how do they get to live like this.

You will never know what is awaiting the corner for you; you don't even know who you might be selling too and what they may be looking to do. They could have another house they don't need and want some kind to live in it. Right time, Right place! Remember to never treat people bad or take your life out on them.

Support comes in many different forms and at many different times. Also, be open to support and to provide support to people around you. You never know who you may need or what you may need.

RESOURCES

NAMI (NATIONAL ALLIANCE ON MENTAL HEALTH)
800.950.6264
OR TEXT "NAMI" 741741

SUICIDE PREVENTION LIFELINE
800.273.8255

THE TREVOR PROJECT
866.488.7386

MCCOY-BROWN INTERVENTIONS (LIFE COACH)
678.637.3410

ABOUT THE AUTHOR

BRODIE PROCTOR

WWW.BRODIESYOURGUY.COM
INSTAGRAM: @BRODIESYOURGUY
FACEBOOK: BRODIE PROCTOR

www.ingramcontent.com/pod-product-compliance
Lightning Source LLC
Chambersburg PA
CBHW071412290426
44108CB00014B/1788